Sunrise Book

# All Times Children's Stories

Tales from Tiny Tots

# Preface

*Welcome to the wonderful world of imagination - of magic, of adventure, of animals that speak, of happenings that are strange and marvellous! This is a series of five books, carefully graded with regard to language and concept. The stories have been adapted from a wide variety of sources - the Panchatantra, Aesop's Fables, the Brothers Grimm, Hans Christian Anderson and folk tales from all over the world. Colourful illustrations bring alive the characters.*

*We hope that through these books, children will discover the matchless pleasure of reading and will embark on a fascinating journey of discovery and delight.*

## Contents




**SUNRISE PUBLISHERS**

32/33A, Street No. 9, Bhikam Singh Colony, Vishwas Nagar, Shahdara, Delhi - 110032 (India)

Tel : +91-11-71218130, Whatsapp No. : +91-7835078000

E-mail : sunrisepub@gmail.com, export@sunrisepublisher.com

Visit us : www.sunrisepublisher.com

**ISBN : 978-81-781305-1-4**

*Printed by* **Tan Prints (India) Pvt. Ltd.,**

Village Rohad, Distt. Jhajjar, Haryana

# 1. The Emperor's Mew Clothes

Once there was an Emperor who ruled over a big kingdom. But he did not care for his kingdom or his people. All he cared about was clothes. He had cupboards full of clothes. But he wanted more and more and more.

One day two tailors decided to teach him a lesson. They set up a big shop in the middle of the town. But they did not let everybody enter their shop. 'We don't sell to ordinary people,' they said.

By and by the Emperor heard of them. He called them to the palace. They refused to come, 'Our cloth is so rare and costly,' said they, 'that we cannot take it out of our shop without guards.'

So the Emperor sent six soldiers. The two men came with them carrying a golden chest. When they were brought before the Emperor, they said, 'We have very rare cloth. Only a good and pure person can see it. If a person has done something wicked, he won't be able to see it.'

Then they opened the casket. It was empty.

`Look at the golden cloth!' they cried. 'See, it has filled the room with light!'

Now no one could see anything for there was nothing to see. But nobody wanted to be called wicked. So they said, 'What beautiful cloth!'

The Emperor couldn't see anything either but he said, `I want a suit made of this cloth.'

So the tailors took a hundred pieces of gold and promised to have the suit ready by the Emperor's birthday.

Soon everyone came to hear of the cloth that no wicked person could see. Everyone was very excited.

On the Emperor's birthday the two tailors brought a big package. 'Carry it carefully,' they said to the servants. `It contains the Emperor's new clothes.'

The servants handed over the box to the Emperor. The Emperor opened it. Of course there was nothing there. But his servants said, 'How beautiful!' and helped him to dress.

Now the people had lined the streets to see the new clothes. When the Emperor came out wearing only his underclothes, they were too shocked to say anything. Each one thought that he was the only one who could not see anything. Just then a little boy shouted, 'But he's not wearing anything!'

Then all the people began to laugh. They laughed so much that tears ran down their cheeks. They saw how they had been tricked. They saw how the Emperor had been tricked. The poor Emperor rushed indoors. How angry he was! And how ashamed! What a lesson he had learnt!

## 2. How The Dog Found Himself A Master

You know that the dog is man's best friend. Well, a long time ago, this was not so. Dogs were wild animals and lived in the forest.

One day one of the dogs decided that it would be fun to have a master. He wanted to have someone to give him food and teach him tricks. Someone who could love him and most important - someone he could love.

So one morning he set out to find a master. He had not gone far when he saw a wolf. It was a huge animal.

`I think Mr. Wolf will make a good master,' he said to himself.

So he walked up to the wolf and said, `Mr. Wolf, would you like to be my master?'

The wolf was very pleased and said, 'I should like that very much indeed.'

So they both walked along for a while. All of a sudden, the wolf stopped and sniffed the air. Then he cried, `Run for your life!'

`But why?' asked the dog. `Who are you afraid of, Mr. Wolf?'

`I'm afraid of the lion,' said the wolf. 'He'll tear me to bits!' Then away he ran!

The dog was very disappointed. 'I don't want a master who's afraid of anyone,' he said to himself.

Just then he saw the lion coming, 'Why don't I ask Mr. Lion to be my master?' he said to himself. 'Even Mr. Wolf is afraid of him.'

So he walked up to the lion and said, 'Mr. Lion, would you like to be my master?'

The lion was very pleased and said, 'I should like that very much indeed.'

Now the dog lived happily with the lion for a few days. One day they were just about to eat when the lion stopped and sniffed the air. Then he said, 'Run for your life!'

`But why?' asked the dog. 'Who are you afraid of, Mr. Lion?'

`I'm afraid of Man,' said the lion. 'He's clever, brave and wise. My strength is of no use against his wit.' Saying this the lion took to his heels.

Now the dog knew what he had to do. He rushed up to the man.

`Mr. Man,' he said, 'I have been searching for someone like you for a long time. Please be my master.'

So man became the dog's master. And ever since men have kept dogs and the dog has been Man's Best Friend!

## 3. The Most Beautiful Woman In The World

It was harvest time. The fields were full of golden, waving corn. Men and women, in their colourful clothes, were busy harvesting the corn. Most of the women kept their young children with them lest they should get lost. Soon it was lunchtime. Everyone sat down to eat. As they opened their lunch packets, they heard a child crying. One of the young men went to see who it was. He came back with a small boy - about four years old. The little boy was crying. 'I want my Mummy .. I want my Mummy!' sobbed the little boy.

Immediately all the people gathered around him asking questions.

'What's your name?'

`What's your Mummy's name?'

`Where do you live?'

But the little boy cried and cried, 'I want my Mummy! .... I want my Mummy!'

Finally one of the women picked him up and tried to quieten him. 'If you don't know your mother's name, tell us, what she looks like - we'll find her for you.'

The little boy stopped crying. 'My mother is the most beautiful woman in the world,' he said proudly.

The men and women laughed. 'Then it won't be difficult to find her,' they said.

Then Ivan, the young man who had found the little boy, called Vanya. Vanya was tall and fair. She had blue eyes and long golden hair. She was the most beautiful woman in the village. She came laughing and blushing, proud to be chosen. 'Ivan, you naughty fellow,' she said, `I know all my children. This is not my son.'

But Ivan asked, 'Is this your mother?'

The little boy took one look at her and burst into tears. 'No! No!' he cried. 'My mother is the most beautiful woman in the world!'

Just then from the next field came a woman. She was short and plump. Her skin was dusky and her hair was streaked with grey. The little boy sprang down from the arms of the person holding him. He flung himself into the woman's arms.

'My little boy,' said the woman, picking him up and kissing him.

The little boy's tears were forgotten. He clung to the woman and beamed proudly at the crowd of men and women.

'See?' he said with pride. 'I told you, my mother was ,the most beautiful woman in the world!'

# 4. The Little Red Hen

Once upon a time there lived a Little Red Hen. She had five little chicks. One day she found some grains of wheat.

`Who will help me plant this wheat?' asked the Little Red Hen.

`Not I, ' said the dog.

`Not I,' said the cat.

'Not I,' said the duck.

`Then I will,' said the Little Red Hen. So she and her five little chicks planted the wheat grain.

After some time the plant grew healthy and strong. It had long stalks of wheat. The wheat ripened in the sun and was soon golden and ready to be harvested.

`Who will help me harvest this grain?' asked the Little Red Hen.

`Not I,' said the dog.

`Not I,' said the cat.

`Not I,' said the duck.

'Then I will,' said the Little Red Hen. So she and her five little chicks harvested the grain.

'I must ask the miller to grind it,' said the Little Red Hen. 'Who will help me take it to the miller?'

'Not I,' said the dog.

'Not I,' said the cat.

'Not I,' said the duck.

'Then I will,' said the Little Red Hen. So she and her five little chicks took it to the miller and brought home the fine white flour.

'Who will help me bake a cake?' asked the Little Red Hen.

'Not I,' said the dog.

'Not I,' said the cat.

'Not I,' said the duck.

'Then I will,' said the Little Red Hen. So she and her five little chicks mixed flour, eggs, sugar and butter. They put the mixture in the oven.

Soon the house was full of the mouth-watering smell of the cake. The Little Red Hen took the cake out of the oven and placed it on the table. She took out a knife to cut the cake.

`Who will help me eat this cake?' asked the Little Red Hen.

`I will,' said the dog.

`I will,' said the cat.

`I will,' said the duck.

'Oh no, you won't,' said the Little Red Hen: 'My five little chicks and I have done all the work. So we will eat the cake.'

She cut pieces of the delicious cake for herself and her five little chicks and never gave a single crumb to the lazy animals!

# 5. Who Is Watching Us

One evening a holy man was returning home late. As he reached his door, he heard a shout, 'Stop!' The holy man could make out four people. He couldn't see their faces. 'Who are you?' one of them called out.

The holy man answered, 'I am what you are.'

When the men came out of the shadows, he saw that they were robbers! They thought that he was a robber, too, because he had answered that he was what they were. Their leader said, 'You can come with us.' So the holy man went along with them.

The robbers had planned to rob a rich trader in the next village. They gave the holy man a whistle. 'You must blow this whistle the moment you see any danger,' said their leader.

Later that night they went to the next village. When, they were just about to enter the rich man's house, the holy man blew the whistle. Immediately the robbers ran out. They did not stop running until they were safely out of the village.

`You warned us in time,' said the leader. 'Now let us try our luck in the next village.'

However, as soon as the robbers tried to enter a house, the holy man again blew the whistle. Once again they had to run for safety without robbing anyone.

This time the robbers were angry. 'Why did you blow the whistle?' they said, 'We never saw anyone! What did you see?'

The holy man said, 'You may not have seen anyone but someone was watching you.'

The robbers were very surprised. 'Someone was watching' us?' they asked. 'Who was watching us?'

The holy man said, 'God was watching you. God is present everywhere.

He sees all we do. How can you do an evil deed when the Lord is watching over you, all the time, everywhere?'

The robbers were shocked! They had never thought about their deeds in this way. They were ashamed of themselves. How could they have been robbing people when God's eyes were on them? They turned to their new friend.

`Who are you?' they asked. 'You cannot be a robber!' When they found he was a holy man, they fell at his feet.

`Help us to become good men,' they said. They left their evil ways. The holy man had changed their lives.

# 6. Why The Bear's Tail Is Short

Have you ever seen the bear's tail? It's so short that it's almost not there at all. Well, once upon a time, it was long and bushy. Then how did it get short? That's a long story.

It was the middle of winter. Two old enemies - the fox and the bear were looking for food. There was nothing to eat. The surface of the lake was frozen so they couldn't catch fish. The farmers had locked their chickens in big, warm pens. So they had no chickens to eat either.

Then the fox saw a fisherman. He had made a hole in the frozen surface of the lake and was happily catching fish. Quietly the fox stole some fish. Then he ran into the forest and began to eat it.

Just then the bear came along. `Mr. Fox,' he said in surprise, 'where did you get such fine fish?'

The fox said, 'Last evening I made a hole in the frozen surface of the lake. Then I put in my bushy tail. I sat there all night. And this morning when I pulled my tail out, I saw these fishes clinging to my tail!'

The bear was very surprised. 'Really?' he asked,

`Well,' said the fox. 'Have I ever lied to you?'

So the bear said, 'Show me the place.'

The crafty fox led the bear to the lake and showed him a corner. 'I sat here,' lied the fox.

So, that evening the bear made a hole in the frozen surface of the lake and carefully lowered his big, bushy tail into it. Then he sat down to wait. Night fell and the lake began to freeze over. The bear felt the pull of the ice freezing round his tail. He thought fishes were pulling it. He was very pleased.

Next morning, the bear tried to get up but his tail was frozen fast in the ice. By then the dogs of the village came and saw the bear. They began to bark excitedly. They frightened the bear. He sprang up with such a jerk that his tail broke in two. The bear yelped in pain and ran leaving his bushy. tail which lay frozen fast in the lake.

And ever since bears have had short tails!

# 7. Honesty Is The Best Policy

Once there lived a poor wood-cutter. Everyday he used to go to the forest and cut wood. Then he used to sell the wood and bring home enough money to buy food.

One day while he was cutting wood on the bank of the river, his axe fell into the river. The poor wood-cutter did not know how to swim. 'Oh dear!' he said. 'My axe is lost! How can I get it back?'

Just then, the clear blue waters of the river parted and what did the wood-cutter see? It was a river fairy! Her eyes were as blue as the deepest sea. Her long flowing hair was spread out behind her like a golden cloud. She wore a glittering crown. The wood-cutter was so surprised that he couldn't say a word. He just stared at her open-mouthed.

`Don't be afraid,' said the lovely creature. 'I am the River Fairy. Why are you so upset?'

`I've ... I've lost my axe,' stammered the wood-cutter.

`Let me help you,' said the fairy. She sank into the water and was back a moment later. She held a beautiful golden axe in her hands. Its blade shone in the sun and the wood-cutter was dazzled.

`Is this your axe?' she asked.

`Oh no!' said the wood-cutter. 'That's not my axe.'

The fairy sank back into the water again. This time she came up with a beautiful silver axe. It shone with the brightness of a thousand stars.

`Is this your axe?' she asked. `Oh no, no!' said the wood-cutter. 'How can a poor man like me own anything so marvellous? My axe is made of wood, its blade is made of iron.'

The fairy smiled. She sank into the water again. This time she returned with the iron axe.

`Is this your axe?' she asked.

The wood-cutter's face lit up. 'Thank you!' he cried. `Thank you! This is my axe!'

The fairy smiled again. 'You are a good and honest man. As a reward you can keep all the three axes.' Saying this she handed all the three axes to the wood-cutter. Then she disappeared into the water.

The happy wood-cutter sold the gold and silver axes. He got enough money to build himself a beautiful house where he lived happily ever after with his family.

# 8. A Narrow Escape

Once a poor grass-cutter was cutting grass in the forest. Suddenly he saw a lion. The man turned pale with fear.

`Don't be afraid,' said the lion. 'I need your help. Hunters are chasing me. Please hide me in your bundle of grass.'

So the man hid him in his bundle of grass and tied up the bundle. Along came the hunters.

`Have you seen a lion going this way?' they asked.

`No, sir,' said the grass-cutter. 'No lion came this way.'

The hunters went on their way and the grass-cutter opened the bundle and let the lion out.

`That was a narrow escape,' said the lion. Now I can eat you in peace.'

`Eat me?' cried the grass-cutter. 'But I saved your life! You must repay good with good.'

`Well,' said the lion. 'The law of the jungle is we always repay good with evil.'

The man begged so hard to be spared that the lion said, 'Let's ask the first three animals that come this way - what we should do. If they ask me to spare you, I'll spare you.'

Soon along came a deer. When he heard the story, he said, The lion's right. He must eat the man.'

A short while later came an elephant. He heard the story and said, 'The lion's right. He must eat the man.'

The lion was very pleased. He licked his lips. Just then there came a fox. When he heard the story, he said, `It's difficult for me to decide because I think the man is not telling the truth.'

`What?' cried the grass-cutter. 'Of course I'm telling the truth.'

`I don't see how you could have hidden such a big lion in your bundle of grass,' he said.

`Of course he hid me,' said the lion.

`I don't believe it,' said the fox. 'I don't see how it could be done.'

`I'll show you,' said the lion eagerly, wanting his dinner. `Hide me again,' he said to the man.

With trembling fingers the man hid the lion in his bundle and tied the bundle up.

`I see that the man spoke the truth,' said the fox. 'But you lied. You must repay good with good, not with evil. Now remain there till the hunters get you!'

# 9. The Demon Of Blue Mountain

Once there was a rich farmer. He had two sons. One day he called his elder son and said, 'The time has come for me to die. All my riches should be divided equally between you and your brother.'

But when the farmer died, the Elder Brother threw the Younger Brother out of the house. He kept all the land and animals for himself. He gave the Younger Brother a tiny piece of rocky land near the Blue Mountain, a dog and a cat.

The Younger Brother did not mind this. He got to work and soon he had cleared his land of rocks and stones. `Now how shall I plough my fields?' he thought. Then he had an idea. He tied the plough to the dog and cat and started to plough his field.

Meanwhile the Demon of Blue Mountain had been watching the Younger Brother. 'What a hard working fellow he is!' thought the demon. But when he saw the dog and cat tied to the plough, he began to laugh. 'Never in a thousand years have I seen such a sight!' he cried. He laughed so much that the mountain shook.

Hearing the strange sounds, the Younger Brother looked up. What a strange sight met his eyes! The Demon had opened his mouth. And inside his huge cavelike mouth was gold and silver! Quickly the Younger Brother climbed up the Blue Mountain, filled his sack with gold and quickly climbed down. He had become rich! When the Elder Brother saw this he asked, 'How have you become so rich?'

The Younger Brother told his story. So the Elder Brother began to plough with the dog and cat. The Demon laughed again. Quickly the Elder Brother and his wife climbed the Blue Mountain. They began to fill sack after sack with gold. One sack! Two sacks! Three! Four! They were so greedy that they did not climb down. The Demon stopped laughing. His mouth closed. The Elder Brother and his wife were shut up in the Blue Mountain.

The Younger Brother was very sad. He began to plough with the dog and cat again. As soon as the demon laughed, he pulled the Elder Brother and his wife out. The Elder Brother said, 'Dear brother, forgive me.'

So they shared the land and the money and lived happily ever after.

# 10. The Magic Pencil

Once there was a little boy called Misha. He was eight years old. One day his teacher called him and said, ` Misha, you've failed in your Maths test again. Work hard or you'll fail in your exams, too.'

Misha went home sadly.

`What's the matter, dear?' asked his mother.

Misha told her what had happened.

` Don't worry,' she said. 'I think you need a bit of magic.'

` Magic!' cried Misha. 'You know magic?'

`Well,' said his mother. 'I have this magic pencil.' She opened her cupboard and gave him a bright blue pencil.

` Here, Misha,' she said. 'Work hard and write your answers with this magic pencil.'

Misha was thrilled. He threw his arms round his mother and kissed her.

` Thank-you!' he cried. 'Thank-you!'

Now Misha studied hard and wrote his answers with the magic pencil. When the results were declared, Misha had come second!

` Well done!' said his teacher. 'I'm proud of you!'

Misha ran home happily to tell his mother the good news. 'And I got 90 in Maths,' he said. 'The magic pencil really works.'

` It sure does,' agreed mother.

Now after this Misha made sure that he did every test with his magic pencil.

Then one day just before the Finals, Misha lost his pencil! One moment it was there on his desk and the next moment it was gone! Misha looked everywhere for it, • but it had simply disappeared.

By the time he came home, he was crying. 'I've lost my magic pencil,' he sobbed to his mother. 'Now how can I give my Final Exams ? I won't give them! I won't!'

His mother put her arms around him. 'Don't worry,' she said. 'Write with another pencil.'

`I won't!' cried Misha. 'I'll fail!'

`You won't fail, Misha,' said his mother. 'I'll tell you why. That blue pencil was not a magic pencil, it was an ordinary one. You needed to work hard and have confidence. You needed to believe that you could do well. So I told you that it was a magic pencil.'

`It was not a magic pencil?' cried Misha.

`Of course not,' said his mother. 'There's no magic in pencils. But there is magic in people who work hard. They always do well.'

So Misha worked hard. He wrote his answers with a new pencil. When the results were declared, guess who came first? Misha!